Leeches, Lampreys, and Other Cold-Blooded Bloodsuckers

BY GAIL LaBONTE

Franklin Watts
New York • London • Toronto • Sydney
A First Book • 1991

Cover photographs copyright © Dr. B. W. Payton and Breck P. Kent

Photographs copyright © : Dr. B. W. Payton: pp. 6, 15; Larry West: pp. 8, 38 top, 48 right; Wellcome Institute Trustees: p. 10; E. R. Degginger: pp. 13 top, 41 top; Robert & Linda Mitchell: p. 13 bottom; Photo Researchers Inc.: pp. 18 (St. Bartholomews Hospital/SPL), 30, 41 bottom (both Biophoto Associations); Animals Animals: pp. 22 top (John Paling/OSF), 24, 48 left (both Oxford Scientific Films), 29 (J.A.L. Cooke/OSF), 35 top (Raymond A. Mendez), 35 bottom, 38 bottom (both Joe McDonald), 43 (Stephen Dalton); Breck P. Kent: p. 22 bottom; Comstock Photography: pp. 29 bottom (Jack K. Clark), 36 (Russ Kinne); Dwight R. Kuhn: p. 50 bottom; UPI/Bettmann Newsphotos: p. 50 top; The Bettmann Archive: p. 58 top; Minden Pictures: p. 58 bottom (Frans Lanting).

Library of Congress Cataloging-in-Publication Data

LaBonte, Gail.
    Leeches, lampreys, and other cold-blooded bloodsuckers / Gail LaBonte.
        p.   cm.—(A First book)
    Includes bibliographical references and index.
    Summary: Examines such cold-blooded bloodsucking animals as the leech, lamprey, tick, and flea.
    ISBN 0-531-20027-2
    1. Bloodsucking animals—Juvenile literature.   2. Poikilotherms—Juvenile literature.   [1. Bloodsucking animals.]   I. Title.
II. Series.
QL756.55.L33   1991
591.53—dc20   91-12620   CIP   AC

Contents

Leeches, Lampreys, and Other Cold-Blooded Bloodsuckers

These leeches, though not furry
and cuddly, are still among the
most amazing creatures on earth.

1 Bloodsuckers- Uncuddly Creatures

Not all animals are furry and cuddly like kittens, hamsters, and some of the other warm-blooded creatures. Almost everyone likes holding these animals close. Some people enjoy handling cold-blooded animals such as frogs, lizards, and even snakes. But if you were asked to handle a cold-blooded bloodsucker like a leech or let a mosquito or flea land on your arm, you would probably refuse. Yet even at a distance, there are many amazing and wonderful things to learn about animals that suck blood.

While people may not want to get close to bloodsuckers, many bloodsuckers want to get close to us. Almost everyone has been bitten by a bloodsucker at one time or another. They are all around us—in the air, on the ground, and in the water.

If you live in certain parts of North America, you may be familiar with the bite of the blackfly. These creatures launch vicious attacks on people in summertime, often at vacation spots such as beaches and parks.

Fleas, mosquitoes, ticks, and lice are common pests. Most people have met them. People who live near lakes and ponds may have met leeches, too. Lampreys rarely attack humans, but many annoyed fishermen have hooked fish badly wounded by these creatures.

Cold-blooded bloodsuckers are parasites, so named because they take their food from the bodies of living creatures. For these animals, blood is an important source of protein, just as meat is for predators such as lions and tigers.

While some predators kill their food, most bloodsuckers do not directly harm the animals they feed on. Sometimes, however, they spread diseases from victim to victim, and some of these diseases can be serious and even fatal. Because of this, some scientists believe that tiny bloodsuckers such as mosquitoes and lice are among the most dangerous animals in the world.

Yet these animals are also valuable in nature. Birds, fish, amphibians, and reptiles eat mosquitoes and other bloodsucking flies. Fish and other animals eat lampreys and leeches. Some people enjoy eating lampreys, too.

At least one bloodsucker, the leech, may prove medically useful. For thousands of years, doctors used leeches to treat illness, not always successfully. Now

Leeches have been used for medicinal
purposes for thousands of years.
This man is being "leeched"
to try to lose weight.

they are discovering important new ways to use these animals in medicine.

Although bloodsuckers annoy us and spread disease, these unusual creatures are remarkable. Though we might not want to cuddle them, we may want to know more about the ways they survive, find food, and affect people. There are many things to learn about these animals, and understanding them can help us avoid becoming their victims.

2 Leeches— Amazing Healers

Hot and sweaty after the long climb, the hikers wade into the cool mountain pond. The slick mud soothes their tired feet. Suddenly, one hiker screams and runs from the water. The others quickly follow. Attached to their legs and feet are many slimy leeches. The leeches have been waiting a long time for their meal of fresh blood. Fortunately, the leeches are harmless, and they are easily removed.

Several hundred species of leeches live on our planet, mostly in water but sometimes on land. (A species is a single kind of animal or plant. Each species has features that separate its members from those of other species.) Leeches can be found in the arctic regions, in the tropics, and in most other areas. Only the driest deserts and a few Pacific islands are com-

Top: Many kinds
of leeches live
in water.

Right: This leech
is feeding on a
human being.

pletely free of leeches. They are especially common in the lakes and streams of Europe and North America. At least sixty different species live in the United States.

Not all leeches suck blood for food. Some species eat earthworms, snails, and insects. Most of the bloodsucking leeches feed on fish and amphibians.

Only a few species prey on humans and other mammals, and very few of these are dangerous. One dangerous kind of leech attacks and blocks the nasal passages of mammals and birds. It may even cause death by suffocation. A species of land leech creeps into homes in Sri Lanka, attacking victims while they sleep. These attacks may cause severe bleeding. Although leeches can spread disease to frogs and fishes, they are not known to pass diseases to people

Leeches are really worms. Instead of having a round body like an earthworm's, leeches have narrow, flat bodies. Some are less than ½ inch (1 cm) long, while others stretch to a length of nearly 20 inches (50 cm). They may be black, brown, green, or even red in color, and they are often colorfully striped or spotted.

The leech's body is divided into sections, or segments. Underneath the front, or head, segments of a leech is a sucker mouth. Several eyes look out from the top of its head. The middle segments contain an enormous stomach for storing and digesting food.

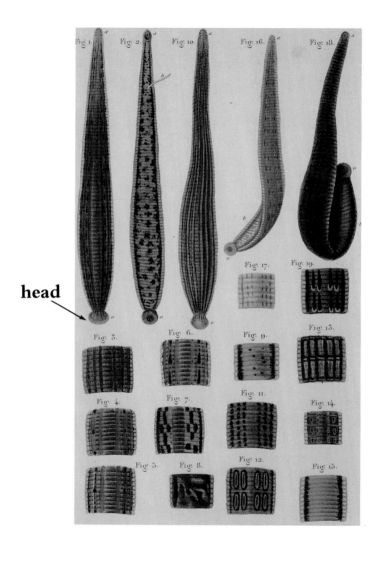

head

The body of the leech is divided
into segments. Underneath the head
segment is a large sucker mouth.

Another sucker, larger than the one on the head, can be found underneath the tail.

Leeches use their suckers in many ways. One way is for locomotion, or moving. A leech moves by looping like an inchworm. After the leech attaches its mouth sucker, its muscles shorten, pulling the tail sucker close to the head. The tail sucker attaches, and the mouth sucker releases. Now the muscles lengthen, and the leech's head moves forward. The front sucker attaches again, and the process repeats, moving the leech slowly forward. A leech that needs to move faster flips end over end, attaching first one sucker, then the other.

Leeches move to escape enemies and to find food. While waiting for prey, the leech attaches its tail sucker to plant stalks underwater or on land. When an animal comes near, the leech senses it in two ways. One way is through the tiny bristles, called papillae, covering its skin. These papillae detect movements in the air and water or on the ground. The other way the leech detects prey is with its eyes. Although its vision is weak, it can see changes in light and dark. After sensing its prey, the leech waves about until it makes contact with the animal. If it is unsuccessful, it may release its tail sucker and swim or crawl toward its prey.

Upon making contact, the leech attaches itself to its prey with its mouth sucker and begins to saw through the animal's skin with its sharp mouthparts. As the leech slits the skin, a chemical in its saliva numbs the wound, and the victim doesn't notice it is being bitten. Another chemical keeps the blood from clotting. Bacteria in the leech's intestines help preserve the blood until it is digested. If undisturbed, some leeches may continue feeding for an entire month.

In one meal, a leech can drink several times its body weight in blood. Then, for six months, it digests the meal. Leeches don't feed often, and some can live for more than a year without eating.

When leeches are three to five years old, they are ready to reproduce. Leeches are hermaphroditic, which means they have both male and female parts in the same body. When two leeches mate, they fertilize each other's eggs. Each leech is both mother and father to the next generation. They lay the eggs in a mucus cocoon, either in water or in damp soil.

After the tiny leeches hatch, they look (except for size) and behave just like their parents. They will survive on the egg yolk for a while; but when it is gone, they will need to find a source of food. For bloodsucking leeches, this source will be blood, and it will be their only food throughout their lives. Leeches are the longest-living worms. One leech was reported to have lived for twenty-seven years!

Despite their slimy nature and bloodsucking habits, there are more reasons to appreciate leeches than to fear them. More than 2,000 years ago, these animals were used to suck the poison out of snake and insect bites. In the 1800s, doctors who thought that "bad blood" caused illness attached as many as fifty leeches at a time to a patient. They hoped that removing the "bad blood" would make the patient well again.

Sometimes the treatment was worse than the disease, and the patient died when his or her sick body was further weakened by the loss of blood. The widespread use of these creatures in medicine was

These medicinal leeches are being used to prevent swelling around an injury.

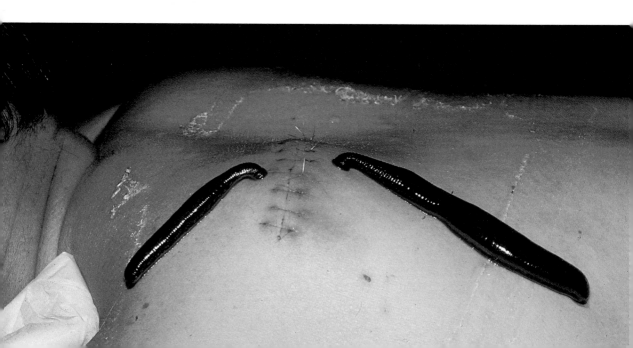

dangerous for the leeches, too. So many medicinal leeches were collected in Europe that they almost became extinct.

Today leeches are making a comeback in medicine. They are being raised on leech farms, and scientists are studying the chemicals they produce. So far, experiments have shown that the anticlotting chemical in the leech's saliva keeps blood flowing freely in human subjects. This chemical may help prevent blood clots that could travel to the heart and cause death. Other chemicals from the leech fight germs and widen veins. Sometimes doctors place these animals on fingers, ears, or other parts of human bodies that were reattached after accidents. The chemicals released by the leeches help restore circulation and speed healing. Leeches also can help heal skin grafts on people who have been badly burned.

Scientists also study the leech's nervous system because the nerves are larger and easier to see than those in other simple creatures. By experimenting with leeches, the scientists hope to learn more about the workings of the human nervous system. One day, in fact, leeches may help us learn how to repair nerve injuries.

Of all of the bloodsuckers, leeches may prove to be the most helpful to humans. Instead of meeting your first leech in a mountain pond, you may someday meet one in a doctor's office.

3 Lampreys—Fishermen's Foes

Long ago, the waters on the earth were filled with life—clams, sea stars, jellyfish, and even leeches—but there were no true fish or any other animals with backbones. Sometime between 400 and 500 million years ago, creatures with backbones appeared in the sea. These were the first jawless fish, and they were the ancestors of today's lampreys.

Lampreys live in the temperate (neither hot nor cold) waters of both the Northern and Southern hemispheres. They do not live in tropical or arctic regions.

All lampreys spend part of their lives in fresh water. Many species—for example, the Pacific lamprey—migrate from the fresh water where they hatched to the sea and back again to lay their eggs.

The Pacific lamprey is common along the Pacific coast of North America from the Aleutian Islands to southern California. A few have been captured near Japan and Mexico. On the Atlantic coast, the American or eastern sea lamprey also migrates from ocean to fresh water, although some of these lampreys have adapted to living their entire lives in the fresh water of the Great Lakes. Species such as the small river lamprey, which inhabits waterways of the western United States and Canada from Alaska to California, never leave fresh water.

Unlike the fishes that appeared later, lampreys do not have biting jaws or scales. They are long eel-like fish with slimy skin. They have round sucking mouths with teeth and sharp tongues.

Lampreys feed on blood only when they are adults. Using their sucker mouths, lampreys attach themselves to the sides of fish and even whales. They open wounds with their sharp tongues, causing the prey to bleed. Like leeches, lampreys inject a chemical that keeps the blood from clotting. When they are full, lampreys leave their victims, which may continue bleeding to death.

Lampreys need the protein and minerals from blood to reproduce. Sometime during their last spring and summer, the lampreys have eaten enough and stop feeding. Now it is time to spawn. For many

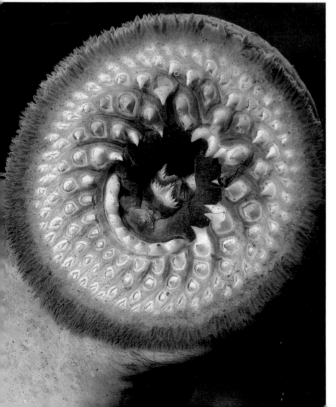

Top: This lamprey is attached to a trout and is feeding on its blood.

Left: The lamprey attaches itself to its prey with a sucker mouth lined with sharp teeth.

lampreys, this is the beginning of an amazing journey.

Sea lampreys must migrate to freshwater spawning grounds before they lay eggs. Some Pacific lampreys travel from the ocean to the headwaters of the Columbia River. They struggle upstream against strong currents for hundreds of miles.

When the lampreys tire, they attach their sucker mouths to underwater stones or logs to rest. They are, in fact, named for this behavior. *Lamprey* is a combination of the Latin words for "sucking stones." Lampreys even use their suckers to climb over barriers and up fish ladders. Only high dams or waterfalls can stop them.

Spawning usually takes place in a shallow, rapidly moving stream. When a lamprey reaches a suitable spot, it prepares its nest. Both males and females attach their suckers to stones and lift and carry them a short way downstream. Their work is done when they have made a bowl-shaped depression in the stream bottom with a pile of rocks at the downstream edge.

Now the male attaches its sucker mouth to the female and wraps its body around hers. As the female releases eggs into the water, the male releases sperm to fertilize them. Many thousands of eggs, about the size of millet seed, are washed into the gravel

Lampreys also use their mouths to attach
themselves to underwater rocks.

and held by the pile of stones. Afterward, these lampreys loosen rocks upstream, allowing sand and silt to wash down and cover the nest. The adult lampreys, weak and exhausted from their work, will soon die.

In nine to twenty days, the eggs hatch and the lamprey larvae emerge. Blind and toothless, they look like transparent worms. In fact, they look so different from adult lampreys that scientists once thought they were a different species.

The larvae are carried downstream, and many are eaten by fish along the way. When they reach an area with a sand or mud bottom, they dig their tails into the river bottom and build tubular burrows. Aiming their mouths into the current, the larvae feed on small organisms and algae they filter from the water. They stay in their burrows as long as seven years.

Finally, the larvae begin to develop into adults in a process called metamorphosis, during which many changes take place. *Metamorphosis* means "to make over" or "to change form." The lampreys develop sucker mouths with sharp teeth and tongues. Eyes appear. The skin turns dark blue on the back and silver on the sides. Fins appear along their backs. The adult lampreys, 12 to 27 inches (30 to 67 cm) long, leave their mud homes and swim freely in search of blood meals.

Although lampreys don't usually attack people,

they are considered a nuisance because they damage fish. Although many fish survive lamprey attacks, many also die from the loss of blood. Lampreys are sometimes a problem when they enter waters where they have not lived before.

Once ships could not travel between the Atlantic Ocean and the Great Lakes because they were stopped by Niagara Falls. In the 1800s, the Welland Canal was built, allowing ships to travel around the falls. The canal allowed the lampreys to make the same journey. In 1921, a sea lamprey was caught in the Great Lakes for the first time. The lampreys multiplied and attacked many species of fish, making some, especially small trout, nearly extinct.

In areas where lampreys have lived for thousands of years, they are not a problem. In the Finger Lakes of New York State, for example, the lampreys have not caused the numbers of other fish to decrease. In fact, all lampreys provide food for larger fish, birds, and even humans. At one time, lampreys were a favorite food of some Native Americans in California as well as a delicacy throughout Europe.

The story of the Welland Canal shows why people must be careful before making changes in nature. No one has been able to rid the Great Lakes of lampreys, but if nature is let alone, the lampreys and other fish there may someday reach a state of balance.

4 Lice-Pesky Passengers

Preschool children huddle together, listening to the teacher read a story. At the same time, a real-life story is taking place on their bodies, but they don't notice. Tiny animals are traveling from one head to another. When the children leave school, they will take these passengers with them. In just a few weeks, these creatures, called lice (one *louse,* two or more *lice*), will multiply into an itchy, crawling mass of thousands. Unlike leeches and lampreys, lice are a common nuisance, and many people have had them.

There are hundreds of species of these small wingless insects throughout the world. Many of them live on mammals and birds. Some of them suck blood, while others feed on dead cells of skin, fur, or feathers. Only three species of lice make their home on humans.

Because lice are small and pale, they are hard to see next to an animal's skin or a person's scalp. Their flat bodies and tough skin make them hard to pick off or scratch away. Long, curved claws at the ends of their six short legs are especially useful for clinging to hair, fur, or clothing. Lice have small, weak eyes and short antennae, so they can't see or sense things far away. But once they are settled in a head of hair, they don't need to explore much. Their food is all around them, just under the skin.

The louse's mouthparts are perfectly designed for reaching its food. First the louse pierces the skin with its tiny teeth. Then it inserts a long, hollow beak through which it sucks the blood. The beak is hidden inside its head when not in use. When the louse is full of blood, it is darker and more easily seen.

As with other bloodsuckers, the protein and minerals in its food are important in reproduction. After mating with a male, the female louse lays ten eggs each day for twenty to thirty days. She glues her eggs to fur, hair, or clothing. Often, people notice the tiny white eggs, called nits, before they see any lice.

The eggs hatch in one week, and the young lice look just like the adults but are smaller. Like leeches, lice feed on blood from the moment they hatch. As they grow, they molt, shedding their old skin and

Right: This human head
louse is clinging to hair.

Bottom: These human
body lice are swollen
with blood from feeding.

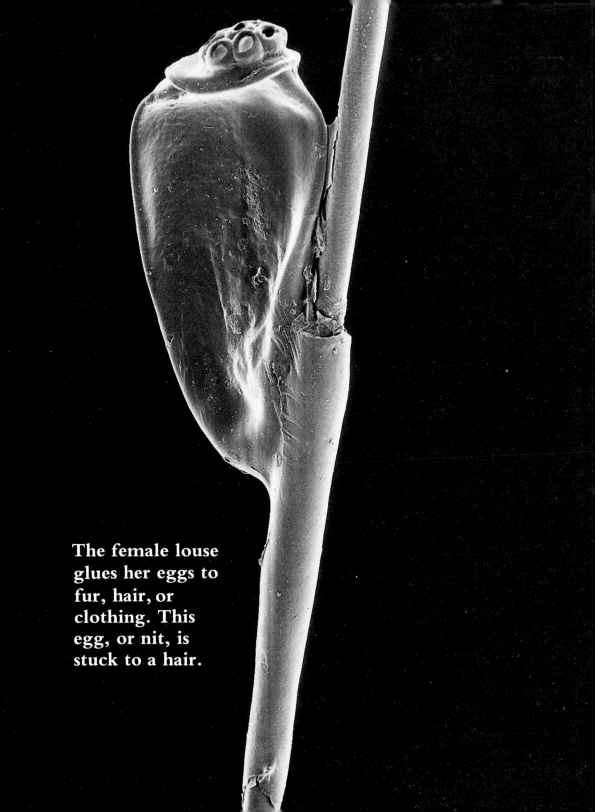

The female louse
glues her eggs to
fur, hair, or
clothing. This
egg, or nit, is
stuck to a hair.

growing a new one. Just a few weeks after hatching, the young lice mate and lay their own eggs.

Usually, lice spend their entire lives, about seven weeks, on one host, the animal from which they feed. But when animals, including people, are close together, lice move easily from one body to another.

Hundreds of years ago, people weren't embarrassed to be covered with lice. People often wore the same clothing for days. Populations of body lice exploded underneath. Backscratchers were invented so that people could reach inside their clothing and relieve the terrible itching.

Sometimes, having lice was considered a good thing. People with lice were thought to be healthy since these creatures would leave a sick or dying person. It was believed that religious people were all the more holy if they could suffer the torment of lice without complaining.

People even thought that lice had special powers. Long ago, in a town in Sweden, a single louse "chose" the mayor. All of the eligible men rested their beards on one table. A louse was placed in the center of the table, and the man whose beard it chose to creep on became the new mayor.

Later, people learned that lice spread typhus and other dangerous diseases. Typhus causes a rash, high fever, and sometimes coma and death. Lice do not spread typhus in the process of sucking blood. Instead, the typhus bacteria lives in the crushed bodies and waste products of lice and enters the victim through cuts or scrapes in the skin. Scratching increases the chances of catching typhus.

Typhus spreads easily when people are crowded together with little chance to wash themselves or change their clothes. Because the disease was common on ships and in prisons, typhus was also called ship fever or jail fever.

Before a vaccine was created, typhus was a terrible problem among soldiers in wartime. During World War I, thousands of soldiers died of typhus. A mild variety of the disease appeared at the same time and was called trench fever, after the trenches in which the soldiers huddled together for protection. The soldiers called the lice cooties, from the Polynesian word *kutu,* which means "parasite."

Lice will probably continue to be an itchy nuisance in the future. However, we are fortunate today to have antibiotics to treat typhus and special shampoos and sprays that put a quick end to these unwanted passengers.

5 Ticks-The Hitchhikers

Anyone who enjoys walking through woods and fields must be careful to avoid another tiny bloodsucker, the tick. All ticks feed on blood, and in the process they spread several diseases such as Rocky Mountain spotted fever and Lyme disease, both dangerous illnesses. Lyme disease, which has been raising concern as it spreads to new areas, is carried by the deer tick in the northeastern United States and by a few other species in other areas. Learning about ticks may help you keep from becoming a victim of this disease and others.

Ticks can be found all over the world, in deserts, forests, and arctic meadows. There are about 1,000 named species of ticks, and each one has its favorite host among reptiles, birds, and mammals.

Ticks are relatives of spiders, scorpions, and mites, all of which have eight legs; insects have only six. Ticks, like lice, have flat bodies and short legs, so they can cling close to the skin of the host animal and not be brushed off. Ticks may be smaller than a pinhead when they have not eaten, but full of blood, they can expand to the size of a small marble.

Ticks can wait a long time for a meal. They may cling to the tip of a leaf for as long as two years waiting for prey. When an animal passes by, the tick stretches out its front legs and catches the animal's fur with its claws; or if the victim is human, it attaches itself to clothing.

After finding a place to bite, the tick pierces the skin with its powerful jaws. It then inserts its whole head into the hole and begins to suck. As the tick feeds, chemicals in its saliva mix with the blood, thinning it and making it easier to digest. The tick also produces a kind of glue to help it stick to the prey for a long meal. The tick may continue eating for two days. It may not eat again for a year. Ticks do not eat often. The deer tick, for example, eats only three meals during its two-year life span.

Deer ticks, like many other species of tick, begin their lives in the spring. They hatch from eggs laid on the forest floor. In their first stage, the ticks have only six legs. At the end of the summer, deer ticks

On the left is
a dog tick.
Below is a dog
tick engorged
with blood.

This deer tick is magnified 100
times. Notice the sharp mouth and
the pincers. This tick seems to
resemble a crab, doesn't it?

take their first meal, usually from white-footed mice. If the mice are infected with Lyme disease, the ticks may take in the bacteria along with the blood.

During their first winter, the young ticks are not very active. By spring they turn into nymphs, the stage before they become adults. Now they have eight legs, but they are still quite small, only the size of a pencil dot. The nymph deer ticks feed for three or four days, usually on mice, dogs, or humans. Again, they need only one meal at this stage, but that is enough to pass the dangerous bacteria to the host animals.

At the end of the second summer, the nymphs molt, or shed their skins, and become adults. Now their favorite food is the blood of the white-tailed deer. As soon as adult ticks eat, they are ready to mate. Male ticks die after mating, but the females live until spring and produce nearly 2,500 eggs. After egg-laying, the females die, too.

Scientists are very concerned about the spread of Lyme disease, which has been reported in forty-three states in the United States as well as in Europe, Asia, and Australia. At first the disease causes flulike symptoms and may cause a rash around the area of the bite. Later the victim may suffer from pain in the joints, fatigue, and fever. Lyme disease can damage the heart, liver, and nervous system, sometimes re-

Right: Deer ticks are very hard to see. Perched on blades of grass, they are easily picked up by animals and human beings passing through.

Bottom: These oxpeckers are hunting and eating ticks off the back of a rhinoceros.

sulting in death. It can be cured if it is treated early with antibiotics.

People should be aware of ticks especially during May, June, and July, when the nymphs are feeding. But the ticks are so small at this stage that they are hard to see. Hikers should wear long-sleeved shirts and long pants tucked into socks. After a walk or hike, it is a good idea to inspect one's body for "moving freckles." A shower is wise, too. If you find a tick, remove it quickly and carefully to lessen the chance of disease or infection. Scientists are trying to create a vaccine to prevent Lyme disease.

Ticks do have some value in nature. For example, they provide food for many birds, including tickbirds, cowbirds, and oxpeckers. In Africa, the oxpecker hunts and eats ticks that it finds on the backs of large mammals such as rhinos, buffalos, and giraffes. The oxpecker helps the large mammals by removing ticks and warning of danger. When the bird sees a lion or leopard, it shrieks and flies away, giving its host time to escape. The tiny tick brings these helpful birds and the large mammals together.

6 Fleas-The Mighty Leapers

How strong would you have to be to jump to the top of a tall building or leap over a city block? As strong as a flea!

With the jumping power of a flea, you could reach the top of a twenty-story building in a single bound or sail over the houses of your neighbors. The flea, however, jumps for more ordinary reasons, including moving from one spot to another, escaping predators, and perhaps most important, reaching food. This tiny, wingless insect uses its leaping ability to jump onto passing animals to obtain a meal of warm blood.

Thousands of species of fleas have been identified throughout the world, including 250 species in the United States. Each species of flea prefers to feed on

Left: Thousands of
species of fleas
inhabit the earth.
Notice the long
hind legs on this
common dog flea.

Bottom: The foot of
a flea (here magnified
over 500 times) is
suited to cling to
fur, skin, and hair.

one species of animal, usually a mammal or bird. But fleas will feed on other animals when their favorites are not available. The flea that dines on humans also dines on pigs.

Fleas find prey by using their antennae and body hairs. They can sense the footsteps, the air movements, and the warmth given off by passing animals, somewhat in the same manner as leeches. And like leeches, fleas have poor eyesight.

While waiting for prey, the flea keeps its long hind legs tucked tightly against a rubberlike pad of material on its abdomen. When the flea releases its hind legs, this material, called resilin, acts like a spring. It snaps the flea into the air with more force than the engines of the space shuttle during liftoff. As it leaps, the flea somersaults over and over with its three pairs of legs pointing in different directions. The flea has been described as a "whirling burr," and like a burr, it sticks easily to animal fur or human clothing.

Once the flea is on board, its narrow body allows it to pass through hair or fur like a coin on edge going through a slot. Its hard, smooth shell makes the flea almost impossible to pick off or crush. It slips out from between fingers or a dog's clenched teeth.

The flea uses palps, or feelers, located below its mouth to find a suitable spot on the skin to take a meal. Then it hammers into the skin with sharp mouthparts and inserts a tube for sucking blood. As it sucks, a chemical from its saliva enters the wound and keeps the blood from clotting. This chemical causes the area of the bite to itch later.

Only adult fleas drink blood, and both males and females need it to reproduce. During the adult stage,

The flea is the greatest jumper on earth. This photograph of a flea "in flight" was taken using special equipment.

which lasts from a few weeks to a year, the fleas find mates. After mating, the female flea lays from 300 to 500 eggs in the fur of its host or on the ground or floor nearby. If its host is human, the eggs are laid in clothing or hair. Out of the eggs crawl small, whitish, wormlike creatures. These are the flea larvae.

For two or three weeks the larvae feed on loose hairs and dead skin cells fallen from the host animals. Then they make a cocoon in which they change into adults. This stage, called the pupal stage, usually lasts one or two weeks, but it can last much longer.

Fleas emerge from their cocoons when they sense warmth or movement. They may remain in their cocoons for a year or more until a warm-blooded animal passes nearby. Sometimes campers entering a deserted cabin find themselves covered in a few moments with newly hatched fleas.

For centuries, fleas have been a source of amusement. The first microscope was called a flea glass because people spent so much time studying these tiny insects through it. At one time, fashionable women wore decorative pendants that were actually small traps with live fleas inside. Some people dressed up dead fleas and put them on display. A museum in Edinburgh, Scotland, contains a whole wedding party of fleas in costume.

Flea circuses were popular in the past. In the 1800s, circus fleas were harnessed to tiny gold chariots which they pulled! Between acts, the owners placed the harnessed fleas on their arms and allowed them to feed.

As well as amusing people, fleas have also caused much suffering. They are responsible for spreading deadly human diseases such as typhus and bubonic plague. Bubonic plague is a very infectious disease that, before the invention of antibiotics, often ended in death. Fleas carry this disease to humans after picking it up from rodents such as rats.

Rats often move when their homes become too crowded or food becomes scarce. As they migrate, the fleas they carry may take meals from other wild rodents. If these rodents carry the plague bacteria, the fleas spread the disease to the rats. As the rats begin to die and their bodies cool, the fleas look for other meal sources. In crowded cities, these sources may be people. The diseased fleas are already dying themselves, their digestive systems blocked with the plague bacteria. But they try to feed anyway, injecting the bacteria into human victims.

Eventually, the disease spreads so fast and to so many victims that it becomes an epidemic. The rats, fleas, and people all die. When the population of each group is small enough, the disease dies out for a while. Today, plague can be cured with antibiotics, but it is still present in some parts of the world, including many wilderness areas in the western United States, where it is carried by fleas on squirrels.

7 Bloodsucking Flies-Aerial Attackers

Flies of all kinds are important in nature. Along with bees and other flying insects, they are pollinators that help plants produce seeds. And flies are nature's janitors, clearing waste and decaying plants and animals from the environment. Many birds, reptiles, amphibians, and fish depend on flies for food.

About 80,000 species of flies inhabit our world, and of those, many feed on blood. Biting and bloodsucking flies can be found in almost every part of the world. From the tiny no-see-um, the size of a pencil dot, to the large horsefly, they attack us from the air. There are bloodsucking sandflies, blackflies, hornflies, deerflies, and, of course, mosquitoes. Yes, mosquitoes are flies, too.

Mosquito is a Spanish word that means "little fly." Mosquitoes are really a kind of blackfly. Nearly 3,000 species of mosquitoes live on earth, from north of the Arctic Circle to the subtropics.

The mosquito is easy to recognize. Although its body is small, it has two wings and six very long legs. Two antennae, or feelers, protrude from the front of its head. Like other flies, the mosquito has two large eyes made up of hundreds of separate lenses.

Both male and female mosquitoes begin their adult lives feeding on nectar from flowers and fruits. This will be the male's only source of food, for it never develops the sucking mouthparts of the female. Between the female's antennae is a long mouth that contains several cutting "tools" and a sucking tube. Females must feed on blood to get protein needed to produce eggs.

The female finds her victims by detecting the carbon dioxide, ammonia gas, water vapor, and heat they give off. After landing on an animal, she finds a soft spot in the skin, cuts through the skin, and begins to feed. If undisturbed, the mosquito will feed for about two minutes before flying away. Like the flea and other bloodsuckers, the mosquito has a chemical to keep the blood from clotting. It is this chemical that causes the bite to itch.

Mosquitoes have many enemies, such as birds, spiders, dragonflies, lizards, and frogs. Almost one-third of all adult mosquitoes are killed each day. If

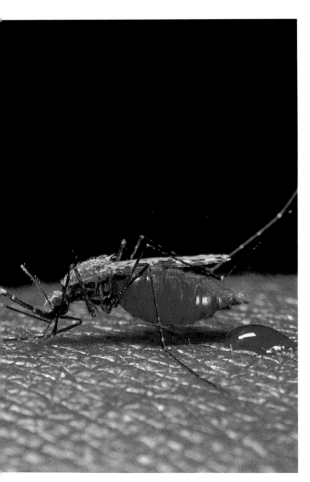 

The picture on the left shows a female
mosquito feeding. On the right you
can see a close-up of a mosquito
feeding through its proboscis.

their species is to survive, mosquitoes must mate within a day or two of becoming adults.

Male mosquitoes have special equipment to help them find mates quickly. The extra hairs on their antennae pick up the high-pitched sound of a female's wings. For each species, the hum is a slightly different pitch. A female in flight will soon be surrounded by swarming males of her own kind.

After mating, the female lays her eggs anywhere she finds still water, which could be a lake, a drainage ditch, or even a tree trunk or old tire in which rainwater has been trapped. During her short life span, usually only a few months, a female mosquito can bring 100 new mosquitoes into the world.

The newly hatched mosquito larva looks nothing like its parents. It has no wings or legs. Its body is long and tubelike. The mosquito larva hangs head down from the surface of the water and breathes through an opening near its tail. Tiny brushes near its mouth sweep microscopic bits of food from the water. The larva has eyes, and if it sees a passing shadow, it quickly wiggles to the bottom of the water for safety.

The larval stage lasts about a week. Then the mosquito enters the pupal stage for a few days. During this time it does not eat. Its body is rapidly changing. Wings, legs, and new mouthparts are de-

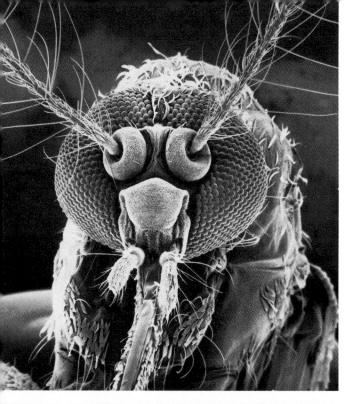

Left: The head
of a mosquito,
greatly magnified

Bottom: Mosquito
larvae hanging
down from the
surface of water

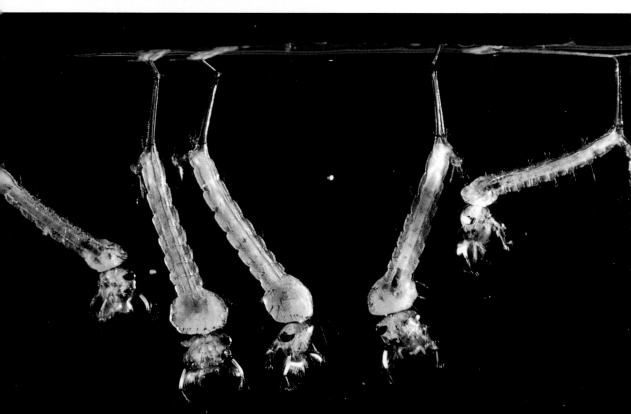

veloping. Finally the pupa splits open, and a full-grown mosquito flies free.

A much larger bloodsucking fly than the mosquito lives in central Africa, from northern Botswana to the Sahara Desert. The tsetse fly looks like a large housefly, but it does not behave like one. Its mouthparts are so sharp that they can penetrate the tough hide of a rhinoceros. Unlike the bites of mosquitoes and many other bloodsuckers, the painful bite of this fly is noticed immediately.

After biting, the tsetse releases a chemical in its saliva that causes the bite to bleed freely. The fly drinks its fill through a beak inserted under the skin. Both male and female tsetse flies feed on blood.

The reproductive cycle of the tsetse fly is unlike that of mosquitoes and most other flies. After mating, the female tsetse does not lay eggs. One egg at a time develops into a larva inside the female's body. When the larva is fully grown, the female rests on a leaf and drops the larva to the ground. Here it burrows into the soil and spends about a month in the pupal stage. At the end of this time, the adult fly emerges and begins to search for food. Tsetse flies feed on the blood of reptiles, birds, and mammals, including humans.

Although there are many bloodsucking flies, only a small portion attacks humans. Of these, the tsetse fly and the mosquito are the most dangerous.

Scientists estimate that mosquitoes have caused half of all of the human deaths since the Stone Age. These insects carry many diseases, including yellow fever, encephalitis, and malaria. Of these, malaria has caused the most destruction. Malaria causes repeated fever and weakness, keeping its victims from working and eventually causing their deaths. It is common in Africa but is also present in large numbers of people in Asia and in South and Central America. Each year as many as 300 million people develop malaria, and about 3 million people die from it.

The tsetse fly spreads sleeping sickness, so named because it causes people to become very tired and eventually to slip into a coma and die. Twenty thousand or more people in Africa catch this disease every year. Many domestic animals such as cows and horses also die from this disease. Rhinos, along with other native animals of Africa, are immune to sleeping sickness.

Sleeping sickness can be cured if it is treated early, but neither medicine nor doctors are available in many of the remote areas where the tsetse lives. Although people have tried to rid Africa of tsetse flies, some believe these insects should be let alone. Because cattle can't survive where the tsetse lives, the land is left as wilderness. For certain, the mosquito and the tsetse fly have kept some parts of the world, especially Africa, from developing as quickly as other areas.

8 *History Lessons*

As small as bloodsuckers are, they have a powerful impact on people. By causing disease, bloodsucking insects have changed the course of history. They have ended wars, destroyed empires, kept some areas of the world poor, and in other areas helped poor people to become rich.

In the past 2,000 years, bubonic plague spread by fleas has struck millions of people in three major outbreaks. The first began in A.D. 451 and spread for two centuries through the heavily populated regions around the Mediterranean Sea. As many as 40 million people died. At the height of the plague, 10,000 people died each day in the city of Constantinople, which is now known as Istanbul, Turkey. The plague played a part in destroying the Roman Empire, one of the largest and most powerful empires in history.

The second outbreak began in the fourteenth century, when trade routes opened between Asia and Europe. In October 1346, ships full of sick sailors and sick rats sailed into Sicily. For five years the disease spread through Europe and beyond, killing 25 million people, one-fourth of Europe's population. This plague came to be known as the Black Death.

Before this time, most peasants worked for rich landowners who paid them only enough to survive. After the plague, few peasants remained alive. Rich landowners had to pay high wages to find workers. With their wages, the peasants began to buy property and develop businesses of their own. Some of them became rich. Others formed what is now known as a middle class between rich and poor.

In 1894, plague appeared again, this time in China. It spread slowly until it reached Hong Kong. Before long, almost 100,000 people in China and Hong Kong were dead. Next it spread to Japan, Australia, southern Africa, and the Americas. Finally, two French scientists identified the bacteria that causes plague. They discovered how it was carried by fleas from rats to people.

Knowing how to control rat and flea populations has prevented any more large outbreaks of bubonic plague. There are still a few cases, but today this disease can be cured with antibiotics.

Der Doctor Schna- -bel von Rom

Vos Creditis, als eine fabel,
quod scribitur vom Doctor schnabel.
der fugit die Contagion
et aufert seinen Lohn darvon.
Cadavera sucht er zu fristen
gleich wie der Corvus auf der Misten.
Ah Credite, ziehet nicht dort hin
dann ROMÆ regnat die Pestin.

Quis non deberet sehr erschrec,
für seiner Virgul oder stecken.
quâ loquitur, als wär er stumm
und deutet sein consilium.
Wie mancher Credit ohne zweiffel
das ihm tentir ein schwartzen Teuffl
Marsupium heist seine Höll.
und aurum die geholte seel.

I. Columbina, ad vivum delineavit   Paulus Fürst Excud.

During the seventeenth century, doctors sometimes wore special costumes during outbreaks of the plague. Could such costumes protect the doctor from getting sick?

Typhus, spread by lice, is another disease that has changed the course of history. Many historians believe that more soldiers have died from diseases such as typhus during wars than from wounds. During the American Revolution, many British soldiers died of typhus and other diseases aboard ships carrying them from England to America to fight. Perhaps the history of the United States would have been different without disease-carrying lice on British ships.

Another bloodsucker, the mosquito, helped the United States in a different way. In 1803, Napoleon, the powerful leader of France, offered to sell the United States enough land to double its size. The Louisiana Purchase was the greatest bargain in United States history.

But Napoleon probably wouldn't have sold the land if mosquitoes had not spread yellow fever to his soldiers in the New World. Napoleon sent 25,000 soldiers to the Caribbean to recapture the island of Haiti for France. All but 3,000 died, mostly from disease. Napoleon decided that keeping control of large parts of the New World was too much trouble, so he sold the Louisiana Territory, including much of the Mississippi River valley, to the United States at a bargain price.

Although Napoleon continued taking over land in Europe, he was eventually overpowered by yet another bloodsucker, the louse. Napoleon sent his soldiers east, to Moscow, to capture new lands. There he was stopped, not only by the severe Russian winter but also by the death from typhus of thousands of his soldiers. Napoleon's empire began to crumble.

Later, France failed in another effort because of mosquito-spread diseases. While trying to build the Panama Canal, the French found they were losing most of their workers to yellow fever and malaria. They were forced to pay as much as $50,000 to $100,000 a year to officials willing to risk working on the project. This was a huge salary at the time. The officials spent their money quickly, living in luxury for a short while before they died of disease. Finally, because the workers were dying faster than they could be replaced, the French gave up and turned over the job of building the canal to the United States.

An American army doctor, Walter Reed, discovered how mosquitoes carried these diseases to people. With this knowledge, Dr. W. C. Gorgas, the surgeon general, took charge of the canal project. He sprayed insecticides on mosquito-breeding areas. He isolated sick people and fumigated their homes. He managed to rid the area of disease in less than two years. Over ten years, the canal was successfully completed.

At one time, malaria was common in the southern United States, southern Europe, and other temperate parts of the world. In 1898, scientists discov-

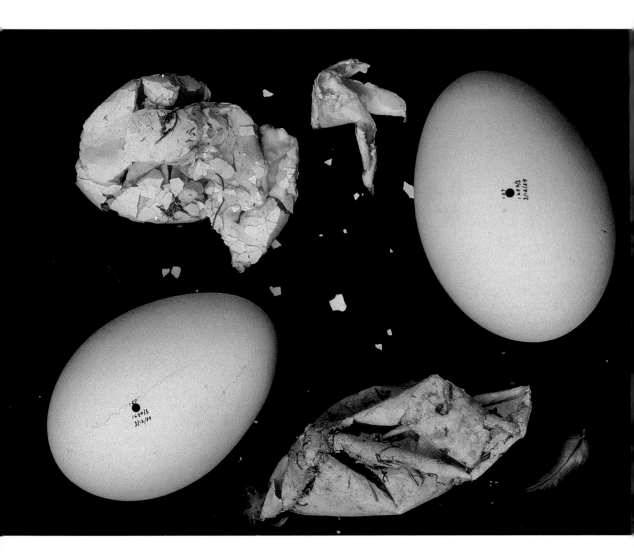

Normal-looking pelican eggs compared with eggs affected by DDT

ered the microscopic organism in the blood that causes malaria. With drugs to treat the disease and chemicals to kill the carrier mosquitoes, the disease was wiped out in many areas. However, the war against malaria in the tropics is far from won.

Sometimes our efforts to fight these diseases have caused more problems. A chemical pesticide called DDT was once used throughout the world to kill mosquitoes, flies, and other pests. But this chemical seeped into the ground and water and then into the food chain.

Birds feeding on fish and insects began to show the effects of DDT. Their eggs were laid with thin and brittle shells that cracked before the baby birds could develop. Some species of birds, such as the brown pelican and the peregrine falcon, nearly became extinct. DDT was destroying birds, some of our best natural pest controllers. Finally, this dangerous pesticide was banned in many areas of the world.

We will probably always share the world with leeches, lampreys, and the other cold-blooded bloodsuckers. Scientists will continue trying to find new and better ways to control the more dangerous species and the diseases they spread. There is still much to be learned about these amazing animals.

For Further Reading

Blassingame, Wyatt. *The Little Killers: Fleas, Lice, Mosquitoes.* New York: G. P. Putnam's Sons, 1975.

Cole, Joanna. *Fleas.* New York: Morrow, 1973.

Halton, Cheryl Mays. *Those Amazing Leeches.* Minneapolis: Dillon Press, 1989.

Hellman, Harold. *Deadly Bugs and Killer Insects.* New York: M. Evans, 1978.

Landau, Elaine. *Lyme Disease.* New York: Franklin Watts, 1990.

Mosquito. Oxford Scientific Films. New York: G. P. Putnam's Sons, 1982.

Moyle, Peter B. *Inland Fishes of California*. Berkeley, Calif.: University of California Press, 1976

National Wildlife Federation. *The Unhuggables*. Vienna, Va.: National Wildlife Federation, 1988.

O'Toole, Christopher, ed. *The Encyclopedia of Insects*. New York: Facts on File, 1986.

Patent, Dorothy Hinshaw. *Mosquitoes*. New York: Holiday House, 1986.

Patent, Dorothy Hinshaw. *The World of Worms*. New York: Holiday House, 1978.

Zinsser, Hans. *Rats, Lice, and History*. Boston: Atlantic Monthly Press, 1963.

Index